WALKING IN LONDON

PARK, HEATH AND WATERSIDE

25 WALKS IN LONDON'S GREEN SPACES

by Peter Aylmer

JUNIPER HOUSE, MURLEY MOSS,
OXENHOLME ROAD, KENDAL, CUMBRIA LA9 7RL
www.cicerone.co.uk

Millrace, Watermeads nature reserve (Walk 19)

which wildlife can flourish, as well as untroubled routes for walkers.

To sum up: London is built on impermeable clays across the centre; porous chalk to the south and north-west; and gravel toppings appear throughout. Each of these, and little local outcrops too numerous to count, combined with the flow of London's many rivers, give rise to different habitats, and contribute to a diversity of wildlife which is still apparent to this day. It may require significant human intervention to maintain it – often in conflict with forces of human self-interest that seek to destroy it – but that diversity is a glory of London. Any Londoner should be proud of it, and any visitor can seek it.

LONDON'S OPEN SPACES

Londinium was tightly enclosed within its walls. After the Romans' departure, that settlement was largely left to ruin, but a new city grew up to its immediate west, and so began the slow development of London.

Slow, that is, until the 19th century, when the city became the largest in the world, and the tight Thames-side site that had served for centuries, barely more than a couple of miles long, simply could not hold the burgeoning population. The railways enabled new suburbs to be carved out of green fields, woods and market gardens, with the last major developments, such as the Metroland of outer north-west London and the great estates around Becontree in the east, taking place between the wars.

And yet, open space survives, by a mixture of private benevolence, public planning, some luck, and the often very active and direct role that Londoners themselves have played.

Although most London open spaces were first created so as to give humans a place to relax rather than wildlife a place to thrive, the two often go hand in hand. It's worth noting, too, that land which is not 'open', such as railway cuttings and derelict industrial sites, not to mention house gardens and allotments, can also be fantastically valuable for wildlife, precisely because human involvement is so limited.

Successive monarchs (and senior courtiers), at least until the 18th century, saw London's hinterland as an opportunity for sport, by which they meant hunting and frolics. Great tracts of land were maintained for that purpose, either as formal gardens such as those around Hampton Court or rougher lands over which men could gallop, nearby Bushy Park an example. But tastes, and pressures on royal time, changed, and the lands became less necessary to their daily needs.

The eleven Royal Parks range from small gardens (and one cemetery) to the famous large expanses such as Hyde Park and Richmond Park. Save for Greenwich Park in the south-east, these are all situated in the wealthier areas of the capital. Much of London's growth during the

Allotments, West Finchley (Walk 12)

19th century, often in cheap housing where crime and disease were rife, took place elsewhere. Many developers no doubt saw open space as just a lost opportunity for profit.

It took government action to create London's first public park, Victoria Park in the east end, in 1842. But such a top-down approach was needed less as first the Metropolitan Board of Works and then the London County Council, with smaller boroughs beneath it, took on the responsibility of providing open space for London's residents.

All around Victorian London there were great natural spaces held as common land. From Tudor times, and gathering great force from the 18th century, tracts of land which

were once open for all to use – for grazing, say – became enclosed by a landowner and the collective rights withdrawn. Although the city had grown in part through the use of enclosure for housing and commercial development, areas right across the capital from Tooting Common to Hampstead Heath and Epping Forest were still held in common. In 1864 the proposed enclosure of much of one of the largest of the commons – Wimbledon – proved a spur to campaigners, who feared that if Wimbledon went, no other common in the capital would be safe. Meanwhile, in Epping Forest, enclosures by a local vicar were opposed by the direct action (and ensuing imprisonment) of his parishioners.

The Croydon tram network features on Walks 19 and 21

get around. Car parking can be very expensive and road congestion horrendous. Even residential areas can have very restricted parking, although things might be easier on Sundays.

Most of the time, London's public transport works fantastically well. There are some excellent smartphone apps, such as Citymapper, which give real-time information, as do the websites www.tfl.gov.uk (tube and bus services) or www.nationalrail.co.uk (National Rail services).

Off-peak services are rarely more than 15 minutes apart; the few exceptions are mentioned on each walk. Sunday services are generally less frequent, and in some cases may not run at all, and engineering works on both tube and rail can lead to bus replacements that take far longer. Check before you go.

If you are a visitor, either arm yourself with an Oyster card (a pre-loaded smart card valid on almost all tubes, trains, buses and trams within London), a contactless debit card (but it's unlikely to be sensible to use cards in foreign currency because of the transaction fee), or use a major mobile phone payment app. All come with a price cap promise, so they are a far better option than buying individual tickets or daily travelcards. Only one walk (Walk 1) starts outside the zonal system, by one stop, but it does take Oyster and contactless cards.

If you can, travel outside the morning peak (peak times are from 6.30am to 9.30am), not least because it's cheaper. Most walks can easily be completed between the morning and evening peak periods, although in summer when it's light (up to 10pm in

June), it's delightful to walk late into the evening.

Children under 11 travel free, and there are significant concessions for 11- to 17-year-olds. If you have a bus pass for England, bus travel is free after 9.30am, but trains and tubes have to be paid for. London residents over 60 get a Freedom Pass for all zones which entitles them to free buses and tubes; almost all trains are free after 9.30am, and some (Overground and TfL Rail) all day.

thickets and bushes just because you think you can.

In farmland, respect the rights of way. Even here there is often a give-and-take between locals and the farmer, and once or twice the walks in this book use a farmland path which is respected in custom and practice. You will also come across a few 'right to roam' areas, shown by a brown logo of a walker traversing rolling countryside, but these are not frequent in London.

ACCESS

England's rights-of-way network gives the walker open access to off-road footpaths, bridleways and other tracks which can lead to the heart of the countryside. They are important in London too, and are often followed in this book. Each is signposted where it leaves a public road, and usually at path junctions as well.

Perhaps surprisingly, London is far more accommodating to wanders off of rights of way than many other areas. After all, most of London's parks and commons were safeguarded precisely because city dwellers were to be encouraged into the great outdoors, and are open to the walker, criss-crossed by a multitude of informal paths. Discretion should be used however – if there's a perfectly serviceable path going in your direction, use it, rather than cause erosion elsewhere, and certainly don't push your way through

WHAT TO TAKE

Good walking shoes or trainers will be perfectly adequate for these walks, except perhaps in winter or after wet weather on the more rural walks that traverse farmland or wood, when proper walking boots will be better.

The shorter walks need almost nothing in the way of specialist clothing, but if you're out for a long half-day or more, look for a wicking top, trousers (if not shorts) that will dry easily (so not jeans or cords), and something warm to pull on when you stop.

If there is any doubt in the forecast at all, take a windproof and/or waterproof layer, preferably breathable. But on most of these walks, you are only a few minutes from a station or bus stop, or pub or café, to take respite from the weather.

If you have a mobile phone, carry it – signal strength is excellent almost everywhere, albeit with surprising

Many walks have fine pubs (Walk 18)

exceptions. Smartphone users will usually find usable 3G signals, or better, and sometimes WiFi hotspots too.

Check the 'refreshments' line in the information box to each walk to decide what food to take with you – although a few snacks are always a good idea, and a bottle of water certainly is, especially in hot weather.

MAPS

The extracts in this book are from Ordnance Survey Explorer maps at 1:25,000 scale. Coupled with the route descriptions, they should keep you on track. London as a whole is covered by sheets 146 and 147, 160 to 162, and 172 to 175.

The OS Landranger series, at 1:50,000 scale, is of less use in London, given how much needs to be

packed in. London is covered by just two sheets, 176 and 177.

Street maps of London vary – some give more off-road detail than you might expect, but in general they won't be using the National Grid that precisely defines start and finish points in this book.

Mapping software allows you to scale Landranger or Explorer maps as you wish and print off specific areas relevant to your walk. Anquet, Quo and Memory Map are three of the best known. All enable maps to be saved to GPS devices, and most to smartphones; ViewRanger is a dedicated app for smartphones.

USING THIS GUIDE

The walks in this book start on the north bank of the Thames east of London and then progress in a roughly anti-clockwise fashion to finish near the Kent border in London's south-east. For each walk there is a plant or animal species described that might be seen on that walk – it might be common, it might be rare, it might be seasonal, but it is in some way relevant to that particular walk. Between them, the 25 species give an indication of the scope of London's wildlife.

A few of the walks stray outside the Greater London boundary, mostly by inches; Walk 1 is the only one to start outside, but even that is within the M25, London's 'second boundary'.

There should be enough detail in the route descriptions, including the map extracts, to follow each walk without using a separate printed map, but it's always good practice to relate the description to the map as you go; this will help make sure you don't go wildly off beam, and also guards against any changes in the waymarking: signs can get overgrown in high summer, for example, and if a sign near housing seems to point the wrong way, it might possibly have been 'adjusted' by local scallywags. Street names in brackets don't have a sign showing that name in the location given by the text.

More to the point, relating to the map gives you a fuller account of the townscape or countryside you are walking through, and not just its shape; the alert map user will spot many details, historic and natural, that the guide can't hope to include.

At the beginning of the route description for each walk there is a box giving a range of useful information: the start and finish of the walk; distance; an approximation of time (see further below); the relevant maps; places to buy refreshments; details of public transport, parking and local interest groups. Some of this information is also summarised in the route summary table. Throughout the route descriptions, place names and features that are shown on the map are highlighted in **bold**.

The estimated walking time is calculated at a fairly relaxed 4km per hour plus an extra half hour – adjust it as you wish to take account of your own speed plus time for a picnic, pub stop or just time spent looking at the flowers. In the route descriptions, a 'minor road' carries very little motor traffic, a rural 'lane' even less and may be unmetalled, while a 'track' is both unmetalled and less robust than a lane.

London has never been a static city. What was in place when this volume was researched may change with the course of time; please see the Updates to this Guide at the front of the book and let Cicerone know if you find that this is so.

Lastly, Appendix A contains details of long-distance paths in and around London, and Appendix B offers details of useful websites and interesting books relating to the capital.

EAST: ESSEX TO THE LEA

Arcelor Mittal Orbit tower (Walk 5)

INTRODUCTION

Eastbrookend Country Park (Walk 2)

Until 1965, the Lea was the boundary between London and Essex, and this boundary had a very real effect on how what is now east London developed. In particular, much of the London-specific legislation preventing noxious industries had no effect here, and so refineries, gas and chemical works, and heavy industry from shipbuilding to railway manufacture were located here instead – especially in what are now its two westernmost boroughs, Waltham Forest and Newham.

Yet wild London was not pressed out of all existence. The River Lea itself became home to reservoirs for London's water, and hence a green corridor for wildlife. Tipping down its gravel ridge between the Lea and the Roding, Epping Forest was saved as London's eastern lung by the steadfast vigilance of locals and city folk alike. The marshes of the Thames below Barking have to this day precluded large-scale development, while further out, town and country battled an uneasy draw that persists to this day.

Walk 1
Rainham Marshes and Coldharbour Point

This is a walk around one of the best places in southern England to see its birdlife. The marshes east of Rainham were formerly used by the military, which kept other users away, and the recent refurbishment of the area by the RSPB is an object lesson in conservation. The walk starts with a circuit of the reserve, just inside Essex, before taking to the riverside, at London's easternmost edge – industry hems in the path, but many species of gull, duck and wader rest and forage here.

The southern edge of the RSPB reserve

Start/finish	Purfleet station (TQ 554 781)
Distance	8 miles (13km)
Time	3½hrs
Maps	OS Explorer 162, Landranger 177
Refreshments	Royal Hotel, Purfleet; café at the RSPB centre
Public transport	Trains every 30 minutes off-peak
Parking	Rainham Marshes RSPB centre, New Tank Hill Road, RM19 1SZ (TQ 547 787)

Turn right out of the station and walk along London Road to the Royal Hotel. Here turn left on a path for a few metres to the Thames, and turn right beside it, passing the **Purfleet Heritage Museum** housed in a former munitions magazine on your way to the RSPB centre. Here, get a ticket to enter Rainham Marshes Nature Reserve – it's free for RSPB members and residents of Thurrock and Havering.

Despite its name, the **RSPB** reserve in fact occupies Aveley marsh. The reserve is open daily except for Christmas Day and Boxing Day. Check www.rspb.org.uk for opening times and entry charges.

Cross the bridge from the end of the café and go ahead at the map sign, soon passing the first and most simple of the hides, known as the Purfleet Scrape. Ignore two left turns at the cordite store – at the second (where there is a little tunnel) go half-right – and also ignore two right turns on a boardwalk. In a little while

you will come to the Ken Barrett hide, a good place to observe birdlife on the adjacent ponds.

Beyond the hide, there is a lengthy boardwalk section through a reedbed, and then a path takes you to the very substantial

The RSPB visitor centre

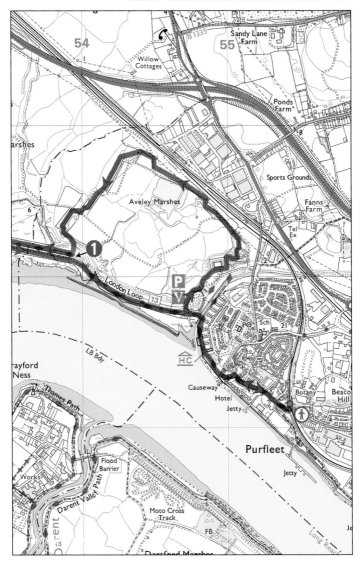

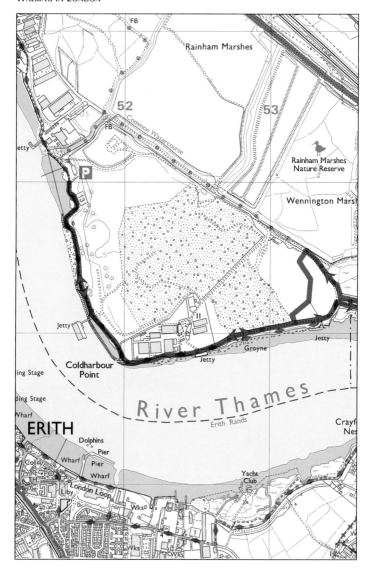

Shooting Butts Hide. Continuing, there is a picnic area to your right, then more boardwalk leads you to a bridge. Here, it's a simple matter to continue back to the RSPB centre, but for the full walk, leave the reserve through the turnstile ❶, and turn right on the path signposted 'Rainham Village'.

THE RESURRECTION OF RAINHAM MARSHES

Rainham, Wennington and Aveley marshes were used as a military firing range for virtually the entire 20th century, thus saving them from other development. In essence, they remained a medieval landscape, and indeed beneath their surface Bronze Age trackways, from a time when the regular flood and drain of the river gave a rhythm to everyday life, criss-cross the site.

To a bird looking for a resting place, or a source of food, even the 20th-century marshes would have looked much like any other wildlife-friendly river estuary. The end of military use gave the RSPB a great opportunity to acquire the eastern part of the marshes in 2000 and to set about restoring habitats such as pools and reedbeds. The bold new visitor centre opened in 2006.

Follow this until it comes to a gap in the fencing on your left, cross the road here, and continue ahead on a fenced path over the eastern tip of the landfill site. This is due for completion in the mid-2020s, after which it too will be actively managed for biodiversity. The path climbs a little to give good views over the marshes, down the Thames estuary, and across Kent, the North Downs in view, and Essex.

Cross the road again and turn right on the riverside path. At **Coldharbour Point**, where there is a navigation light, the river swings from west to north, bringing Shooter's Hill and the Canary Wharf financial district into view. In about 1km you reach the cement barges – around a dozen of them, remnants of a fleet of 500 used in the D-Day landings; they too are a favourite place for birds to rest. The large building in front of you is the Tilda Rice factory.

The stretch from the cement barges to Purfleet station forms the last 3 miles of the **London Loop**. This 150-mile long-distance path, essentially the walker's M25, starts just over the river at Erith Pier, barely a mile across the Thames – but 10 rewarding days or so for the keen walker.

Retrace your steps back past Coldharbour Point and keep on by the river until just before a gate to a small car park. Here turn right on a gravel path to access the sea wall, and stay on it for the views, perhaps venturing over towards the Thames-side saltmarshes. Once back at the RSPB centre, you can either go in, perhaps returning to one or two of the hides, or continue over the bridge over the Mardyke back to the station at **Purfleet**.

WATER PIPIT, *ANTHUS SPINOLETTA*

Photo: Russ Sherriff

On a typical winter's day, there might be 200 water pipits across England, and there's a good chance that a score of them will be dotted about Rainham Marshes.

Unlike rock and meadow pipits, the water pipit is only ever a winter visitor to these shores, arriving from the mountains of central and southern Europe in the late autumn and staying to the spring. Rainham is one of its few overwintering sites in England with the remainder being elsewhere in the south and east. It favours marshy sites but can also be found on flooded fields and places such as sewage works.

The water pipit returns to mainland Europe to breed but it might be possible to see it in breeding plumage just before it does so; it then has a pinkish breast and grey head. Normally it is greyish-brown above and pale below with a pale stripe over its eye.

It is difficult to distinguish a water pipit from a rock pipit, and indeed the two were once thought to be the same species: look for the white outer tail feathers when in flight, which the rock pipit does not have. Rock pipits can be found at Rainham, but they prefer the rougher coasts of western and northern Britain.

Some 500 metres from the road turn right over the canal and then left on a grass path, which bends to cross just below the slightly higher ground to your right that housed Dagenham Hospital until 1989. Turn left on a gravel path when you meet it, cross a footbridge, and turn right on the embankment ❹ of the Wantz Stream.

The gravel path ends mysteriously a few metres from a bench – go to the bench and turn right on a surfaced path. Follow this to a pelican crossing at Ballards Road (**B178**) and go ahead down Church Lane, which turns right in 150 metres. Enter the churchyard, known as 'God's Little Acre' (in fact it is two), of St Peter and St Paul Church, and wander through it to the **church**, which forms an attractive group with the Cross Keys pub and the war memorial. Turn right here along Exeter Road, turn right on footpath 29, and at the end of Dewey Road turn left for **Dagenham East tube**.

BLACK POPLAR, *POPULUS NIGRA*

Like most species of poplar (and other common British trees such as the willow and the holly), the black poplar is a dioecious tree: some trees are male, others female, and therefore they need to be close to each other to pollinate and hence reproduce.

Female black poplars are less common in Britain than male black polars; there are as few as 600, although there are 10 times as many males. The six black poplars in Dagenham are all females, with no male trees for many miles (although there are some on the Lea, in Walks 5 and 6). They are therefore an isolated population that will grow no further, although cuttings from them were planted in South Norwood Country Park in the 1990s.

Look for the yellow-green catkins (those of the male are red), which appear in the early spring. Its triangular leaves help distinguish it from the more common white poplar, which has five-lobed leaves.It may look as though the Dagenham trees are in danger of falling, as their trunks are at an angle. However, this degree of lean is a characteristic of the species. Equally typical are the 'bosses' or burrs on the trunk, which is grey-brown and deeply furrowed.

Walk 3

Epping Forest from Chingford

Epping Forest sits on a slowly rising gravel bank between the rivers Roding and Lea, and stretches from the inner London borough of Newham in the south to well into Essex in the north. It's been an essential place of rural escape for east Londoners since mid-Victorian times. This walk skips both sides of the present London boundary, and shows off a wide range of its habitats – pond and stream, wood and clearing, bog and plain.

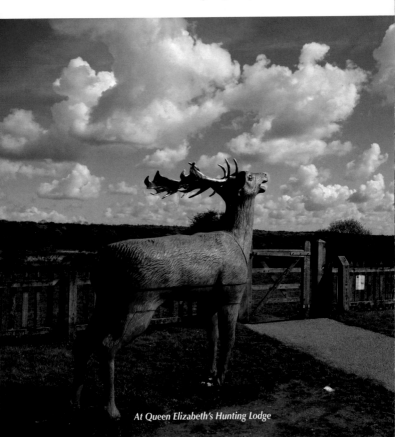

At Queen Elizabeth's Hunting Lodge

ARTIST'S BRACKET FUNGUS, *GANODERMA APPLANATUM*

The bark of a tree is its first defence against damage. It's living tissue, unlike the older heartwood at the tree's centre. But if the bark becomes wounded, say by fire or frost, deer or man, fungal spores can enter, slowly rotting away the heartwood, and in time perhaps hollowing the trunk entirely. Weakened, the tree may topple to give opportunity for new growth, be it tree or insect – see for example the lifecycle of the stag beetle, Walk 17.

One type of such fungal invasion gives rise to the artist's bracket fungus, which might well be seen on older beech and hornbeam trees in the Forest. As the bracket grows each year (it will live at least as long as the afflicted tree, so quite likely a decade or more), it lays down rings, mimicking the tree's behaviour. The fungus itself is a 'white rot', turning the heartwood moist and spongy.

The artist's bracket fungus is immune to the forager's knife. Even if it could be prised off, it is rock hard, and no matter what the cooking would break teeth before it could do any damage to the stomach or brain. It can, however, be carved, hence the name.

Walk 4

Wanstead Flats and Park

This, the southernmost section of Epping Forest, has a fascinating human history, of which the fate of the great house at Wanstead Park is just one facet. It also boasts a remarkable biodiversity. Although part of the area is managed for football, there is also an acid grassland Site of Special Scientific Interest (SSSI) here, plus the Forest's southernmost woods and a complex water system in the former ornamental grounds.

The ornamental waters

Start/finish	Forest Gate station (TQ 404 853) or Wanstead Park station (TQ 405 856)
Distance	6 miles (10km)
Time	3hrs
Maps	OS Explorer 174, Landranger 177
Refreshments	Pubs and cafés in Forest Gate, tea hut in Wanstead Park
Parking	Centre Road car park, E7 0DL (TQ 405 861)
Local group	Friends of Wanstead Parklands www.wansteadpark.org.uk and Wren Wildlife and Conservation Group www.wrengroup.org.uk

Cross the road in front of Forest Gate station and walk to the railway bridge, where Wanstead Park station is situated for those arriving by Overground. Keep walking to the junction with Capel Road, where you cross over to a drinking fountain and enter Epping Forest land. Keep on along a narrow track on **Wanstead Flats**, not far from the main road, until Centre Road car park. This is where car drivers will start.

Advisory sign on the Flats

Cross the road here, at a refuge, and at a gate just to your right look for the path running diagonally. Keep on to cross another road and continue along the right-hand edge of playing fields until a lime tree avenue comes in from the left ❶. At the path junction here, follow the prominent forest ride heading half-right, inside one of the southernmost woods of the Forest, **Bush Wood**. In just over 200 metres, turn right at a path crossroads, coming out to a road (Blake Hall Road) at a bus stop. Cross at the pelican crossing just beyond and enter **Reservoir Wood**.

The path through the wood comes out into **Wanstead Park** at the first of its ponds, Shoulder of Mutton pond, and soon passes another, Heronry Pond. Keep them both on your right, and they lead you to a path junction with an avenue of sweet chestnut trees, leading you towards the Temple, the only intact remnant of the great house's estate. The Temple has information on the park and is open at weekends and bank holidays. But just before you reach the Temple, go left through posts on a path beside Chalet Wood, locally famous for its magnificent springtime bluebells. The path merges on to a track.

A NEW PARK FOR LONDON

Before London's bid for the 2012 Olympic and Paralympic Games, the semi-industrial area of the Lower Lea near Stratford seemed an unlikely place for biodiversity. Oil, tar, arsenic and lead polluted ground and water alike, while those plants that did thrive were often invasive and damaging. Dozens of electricity pylons littered the site.

The two-part clean-up first provided a clean and welcoming site worthy of the world's attention for the intensive month of the Games, and then converted that site into a mix of open space, housing and business. Those two latter elements will not be complete until well into the 2020s, but the 220ha Queen Elizabeth Olympic Park has been opened in stages since 2013. There are two broad areas: in the north, a riverine landscape with wetland habitat and 6ha of woodland; and in the south, formal gardens.

It's worth checking an events diary before visiting the park, for it can get very busy, especially when West Ham Utd are playing at home or a major athletics meet takes place.

Continue until steps force you up to a concourse (Mandeville Place). Go through it, and just after a sculpture of brick pillars veer left. After a playground you pass the 2012 gardens, which showcase plants from Europe, North America, Asia and the southern hemisphere. The London Stadium, as the former Olympic Stadium is now known, became the home of West Ham Utd in 2016 and hosts concerts and major athletics meetings. Just before the Podium café, turn right over grass and drop down to another waterway, the City Mill River. Turn left beside it. Later go up steps

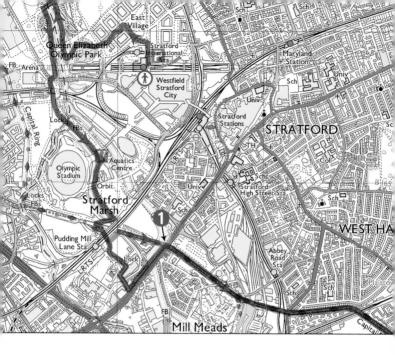

on to a road, cross it at a zebra crossing, and take a ramp up to the Greenway, the yellow-green Viewtube café just on your left, and take the ramp heading down.

Keep on the left side of the road underneath the railway. At the time of writing, a stretch of the Greenway south of the railway was closed so follow the road as it curves right then left until you come out to Stratford High Street. Turn left, and cross the road by a pelican crossing where you see the closed portion of the Greenway coming in ❶. If it has reopened, take the ramp back up to it, and continue to the busy Stratford High Street.

In mid-Victorian times, **pollution of the Thames** was so bad that in 1858 Parliament had to be suspended because the stench from the river was so overpowering. This 'Great Stink' led to calls for a solution, answered by engineer Joseph Bazalgette. He advocated two great sewers, one across north London, another in the south, funnelling waste away from the Thames until it could be treated well to the east of the capital. The Greenway footpath runs on top of the northern sewer – it still functions, with great efficiency!

Start	Tottenham Hale station (TQ 344 895)
Finish	Bromley-by-Bow tube (TQ 380 825)
Alternative finish	Victoria Park (TQ 358 834)
Distance	7 miles (11km)
Time	3hrs
Maps	OS Explorer 174/162, Landranger 177
Refreshments	Ferry Boat Inn and Engine House café near the start; Princess of Wales pub, Lea Bridge; weekend café at Three Mills
Parking	Walthamstow Wetlands car park, Forest Road, N17 9NH (TQ 349 893)

From Tottenham Hale bus station next to the train station, turn left onto the main road (Ferry Lane). Cross at the pelican crossing and continue over first the Lee Navigation and then the River Lea, entering the Walthamstow Wetlands along a metal boardwalk to the Engine House.

Diversion avoiding the Wetlands
The Wetlands are closed after 5pm (or dusk in winter), so if you are starting late, shortly after Jarrow Road turn down the slope on the right to join the navigation towpath. Later, you walk beside Markfield Park, which has a café. At the entrance to Springfield Park (another café), cross the footbridge and continue along the metalled lane, which leads you under a railway – beware the five foot headroom! Continue past a small car park and turn right through a kissing gate ❶ near an electricity pylon.

To continue on the main route, from the Engine House cross a bridge and continue on a footpath on a bank between **reservoirs**. At the end of the reservoirs, turn sharp right over a concrete bridge and then sharp left, passing a footbridge to the Coppermill Tower – well worth a climb to its viewing platform – and then cross another footbridge on your left to come out on to Coppermill Lane. Go through the kissing gate ❶ near an electricity pylon.

The heron is a common waterbird on the Lea

The **Walthamstow Wetlands Nature Reserve**, which opened in 2017, has improved access to a previously isolated and almost secret patch of wild London. Its 10 reservoirs are still one of the major storage points for London's water supply and remain both the largest fishery and the largest heronry in the capital. New reedbeds created for the reserve have broadened the diversity not just of birdlife – look for little egret, shoveler, pochard and gadwall – but of invertebrates and amphibians too.

After the kissing gate, turn left in 25 metres and then left again when you meet a metalled path. This takes you under more rail tracks, this time with wildlife murals to guide you. Continue on a covered aqueduct before turning right at a signboard, first across grass and then on a boardwalk through **Walthamstow Marshes**, still a grazing marsh on which you might see Belted Galloway cattle. Where the boardwalk ends, turn left on a gravel path by the river.

Cross King's Head Bridge on to the towpath, now by a new housing development, and go under the busy Lea Bridge Road, with the Princess of Wales pub on the other side. The towpath switches sides again at the next footbridge and here enter the Middlesex Filter Beds ❷. Inside, turn left to see the 'Hackney Henge', an installation of 1989 by sculptor Paula Haughney using reclaimed granite from a pumping station. Follow a concrete embankment, cross a circular area, and then turn half-right to leave the Beds.

The **Middlesex Filter Beds** were built in 1852 to clean London's drinking water and help stem the recurrent cholera epidemics which then blighted the capital. They worked by continually filtering water from the Lea over sand and gravel, and remained in use till 1969. Since then, nature has done a grand job in reclaiming the site: it's a good place to find mosses and liverworts. Less happily, unpleasant invasive species such as giant hogweed are present too, but from here, kestrel and sparrowhawk hunt over nearby Hackney Marshes.

Middlesex Filter Beds

Outside, turn left on a metalled path which heads over to join the **River Lea** proper (ignore the bridge). The path soon enters woodland and if you prefer you can take an informal path right by the river instead. Just after the next bridge, go through a car park and past the changing rooms for the pitches of **Hackney Marshes** to a road. Cross it at the refuge and enter **Wick Woodlands**. The woodlands were planted in 1996 as partial recompense for the environmental depredations caused by the A12 link road. Turn right on a path and later turn left on the woodlands' superb avenue of London plane trees, planted in 1894 to celebrate Hackney Marshes being taken into public ownership. At the end of the avenue, rejoin the Navigation towpath just before a bridge bearing the very busy A12.

After the bridge you enter the **Queen Elizabeth Olympic Park**, the former press centre beside you. Walk 5 explores the Park in more detail. A few metres after going under the railway bridge, you pass under the Carpenter's Road Bridge ❸.

Alternative finish

This route can be combined with the Regent's Canal walk (Walk 7) to make a 14-mile tour of London's waterways. Cross the Lea Navigation at the Carpenter's Road Bridge ❸, so that it is on your left for a short while, until you swing round right on to the **Hertford Union Canal**. This goes under the busy A12, and a pair of **locks** soon after. At the second of these enter **Victoria Park** through Lock House Gate, but in the park stay near the canal until a road cuts through it. Cross the road (Grove Road) and head to the café by the lake in front of you to join Walk 7.

From Carpenter's Road Bridge, with the Lea Navigation still on your right, you soon come to the Old Ford Lock. To continue to Bromley-by-Bow tube, take the footbridge half-left, signposted for the Capital Ring. After crossing under a low bridge don't follow the Ring up to the left but stay by the river.

As you approach the Bow flyover (A11), cross the river on the new wooden bridge, which leads you under the busy road. A more industrial area follows briefly, but soon the magnificent Three Mills appear on the left. Cross the bridge to them – there is a pleasant small piece of green here ❹.

The **House Mill** is the largest tide mill in the world. Built in 1776, and rebuilt after a fire in 1802, it continued to operate until 1941. There are tours of the mill on summer Sunday afternoons, and the café is open on weekends.

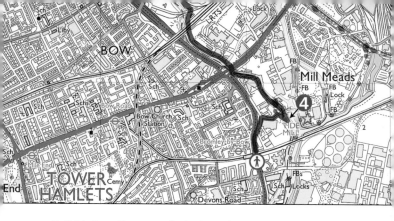

To finish the walk, re-cross the bridge and turn left after Tesco. Go along the busy road, then under it by a subway, and **Bromley-by-Bow tube** is just at the top of the steps.

GRASS SNAKE, *NATRIX NATRIX*

Photo: Gill James

Although the grass snake's name might imply a preference for dry locations, its Latin name – probably derived from *natare*, 'to swim' – gives a better clue to its preferred habitats. For in fact the grass snake is an accomplished swimmer, and there are many records of it in the River Lea as well as by its banks and in the wetlands adjacent.

Females are typically around one metre long, but males barely half that. In colour they can look olive-green or perhaps grey-brown, with a yellow collar – this helps distinguish them from the venomous adder, which also has a black zigzag on its back. However, the young of the Aesculapian snake, of which there is a colony by the Regent's Canal, also have a yellow collar.

Although harmless to humans, the grass snake is certainly not harmless to frogs, toads, fish and small rodents. These are swallowed whole, head first and usually alive. A suitably large meal could last the snake many days if not weeks. All reptiles hibernate in the winter months and the grass snake is no exception, choosing anywhere where freezing might be avoided – from tree roots to compost heaps. Humid places such as compost heaps are also favourite spots for egg-laying.

NORTH:
LEA TO BRENT

Hampstead Heath Extension (Walk 11)

INTRODUCTION

Autumn in Enfield Chase (Walk 7)

With the historic core of both Westminster and the City of London fronting the Thames waterfront, this section contains the heart of tourist London, the Royal Parks its best known green spaces. But heading north, there is more to discover, even before you reach the green belt and the Hertfordshire border.

Hampstead Heath is the great survivor, and without doubt one of the great open spaces of the capital – arguably, the best within such a short distance of the centre. Although there are many good local parks and a few woodland patches to choose from, there is nothing to match it in this section until the more open country around Totteridge and Enfield Chase is reached, some miles to the north.

So a good way to explore this area is to use the wildlife corridors that have been formed by man or nature. Dollis Brook, a Brent tributary, is largely free of development, while that remarkable Stuart-era survivor the New River and the more modern Regent's Canal show how artificial watercourses can enhance city landscapes.

At Alexandra Palace, one of London's few abandoned railways ends in one of the great panoramas to be had from the capital.

he later used to good effect in mining ventures in his native Wales (that later subsidised the loss-making river) and land reclamation on the Isle of Wight. In 1622 he was granted a baronetcy, the first engineer to be so honoured.

At the end of Petherton Road, cross the main road by a zebra crossing ❸ and continue down Aden Terrace, beautifully-kept allotments beside you. Turn left where it ends, and right by the New River Café, entering **Clissold Park** just before Stoke Newington church. Beyond Clissold House, built in the late 18th century for Quaker and anti-slavery campaigner Jonathan Hoare, turn left by the ornamental water, another relic of the original New River course. Cross it by the second footbridge, continue to the Pump House, and turn right. At the end of the park, join the main road (Green Lanes).

When you reach the **Castle Climbing Centre**, turn right on to the waymarked Capital Ring, soon crossing over and continuing beside the New River. The climbing centre is housed in a former New River pump house. To your left is the vast Woodberry Down estate – monolithic post-war tenements now being replaced by still large but more graceful developments – and on the right are the twin **West and East reservoirs**, which store much of the New River's water. The second is now the site of **Woodberry Wetlands**. Enter the Wetlands and walk around the reservoir's southern shore to enjoy this excellent natural regeneration project. Leave by the east entrance, cross a footbridge, then turn right ❹ on a path by the New River. The Wetlands close at 4.30pm daily, after which instead simply keep to the path on the reservoir's northern shore.

WOODBERRY WETLANDS

The Woodberry Wetlands were opened by the London Wildlife Trust in 2016, the first of two wetland projects in north-east London (the second is the Walthamstow Wetlands, Walk 6). When opened in 1833 the reservoir here was 6m deep, but continual silting has cut that to 2m, enabling the reedbed to extend out from the perimeter to the benefit of wildlife.

As well as 17ha of reed-fringed ponds and dykes, there is grassland, hedgerow, meadow and orchard. At least 50 species of bird breed here: warblers in the reed beds, finches and tits around the outside. It's a good site too for moths (including the large spotted leopard moth), butterflies (such as the Essex skipper and purple hairstreak), dragonflies and damselflies.

You soon come to the busy Seven Sisters Road, where you cross the road by a pelican crossing to your right before rejoining the river. On this stretch, you can see how the river contours round an edge of a small escarpment dropping down to the Lea valley, Alexandra Palace clearly in view. Crossing Green Lanes one last time, enter **Finsbury Park**, and follow the Capital Ring signs through it, leaving the river behind. You leave the park by a footbridge over the railway. For Finsbury Park station, turn left at the footbridge. If joining the walk from the station, enter the park by the railway bridge and stay on the left edge of the park.

Turn right on to the Parkland Walk, which follows the richly-wooded trackbed of an old rail line for about 1½ miles.

The **railway line** opened in 1873, to link the new Alexandra Palace to the main line at Finsbury Park. A plan to transfer the route to the Northern Line in the 1930s was thwarted by war, after which traffic declined. The line closed to passengers in 1954, and to all traffic in 1970.

A boarded tunnel ❺ then forces you slightly left up to Holmesdale Road. Continue uphill to crossroads, where turn right on to Shepherd's Hill, then at **Highgate Library** turn left on to a path. Reaching a road (Priory Gardens), turn right, then turn left on a path by the un-numbered house number 10, entering **Queen's Wood**.

Queen's Wood

Capital Ring signs lead you over a road and past a café to another road. Cross it to enter **Highgate Wood** at New Gate, turning right, still on the Ring. At an asphalt track look for the commemorative plaque to the opening of the Capital Ring. Turn left at a drinking fountain to **Bridge Gate** ❻. Turn right just before it, leaving the Ring, to stay inside the wood a little longer. Exit at Cranley Gate, and turn left, dropping down the slope back on to the old rail line. This brings you out to the Muswell Hill viaduct.

From **Muswell Hill viaduct** there are superb views – to the left, of the suburb of that name, and to the right a wide panorama encompassing the City, Docklands, Shooter's Hill, the Olympic Park, the Langdon Hills of Essex and Epping Forest.

Continue through a foot tunnel and enter Alexandra Park. Past a café, continue downhill to skirt a car park – the one recommended if you are doing this walk by car – on the right. Cross a broad path and **Alexandra Palace** appears dramatically in front of you. How could something so massive have been hidden for so long?

Alexandra Palace was opened in May 1873, only to burn down 16 days later. Nevertheless it was rebuilt within two years and has played a major role in London's entertainment scene ever since – despite a further fire, which forced its closure during most of the 1980s. Known to Londoners as the more informal Ally Pally, it was also the site of the first BBC television transmissions in 1935; broadcasting continued until the 1980s, and the antenna is still used for radio broadcasting.

Walk up to and round the terrace – which has another wonderful view, this time broadening out southwards – to the second set of steps descending from the main facade. Cross a road, descend more steps, turn left and almost immediately go down seven more steps. Descend across the grass to a broad track (half asphalt, half gravel) on which you turn left. A few metres after joining a road, turn right on a footbridge to **Alexandra Palace station**.

RED-EYED DAMSELFLY, *ERYTHROMMA NAJAS*

Photo: Paul Ferris

There's perhaps no more evocative sight of the English summer than a dragonfly on the wing, its tissue of wing surely too fragile to keep it aloft. But is it a dragonfly? Or a damselfly? Damselflies are generally smaller, with wings roughly equal in size and shape, while the hind wings of a dragonfly are usually shorter and broader than its fore wings.

If not flying about (roughly between May and August), the male red-eyed damselfly might be seen sitting on floating vegetation, ready to defend it against all-comers. It's more robust than some damselflies, but only the male has the large, deep red eyes that give it its name; those of the female are green-brown.

This adult form is only the short (probably only a week or two for any individual) final stage of the insect. Eggs hatch into larvae that will live under water for a year, moulting as they grow, the final moult into adult taking place above water. Adults eat other flying insects, such as midges and mosquitoes, while the larvae often eat other, smaller larvae. In turn adults are the prey of birds, spiders, frogs and even dragonflies, while the larvae are consumed by diving birds, fish and amphibians.

Walk 10

Royal Parks

The Royal Parks of London's West End, plus Regent's Park a little to the north, are among the best-loved attractions of the city for locals and visitors alike. Between them they form an arc of open space in which it's possible to wander for hours across acres of grassland and through arcades of great trees, all within touching distance of theatres, galleries, shops and palaces. This route takes you through five Royal Parks, passing many of their main attractions to give a good day out in the green heart of the capital. This walk could be split into two shorter walks, breaking the route at Lancaster Gate, a little over half way.

St James's Park

THE ROYAL PARKS

Under the Crown Lands Act of 1851, eight royal parks became public open space, although they remain the property of the Crown. They are run by the Royal Parks agency, which also manages five other open spaces and one cemetery: Richmond Park (Walk 17) and Bushy Park (Walk 16) also feature in this guide.

Each Royal Park has its own distinct ambience. Hyde Park, for example, with boating on the Serpentine and both concerts and public speaking at the Marble Arch corner, has plenty of more-or-less-organised entertainment, while Green Park is a place of transit. St James's Park functions both as a prelude to Buckingham Palace visits and as a lunchtime retreat for civil servants in the nearby government buildings.

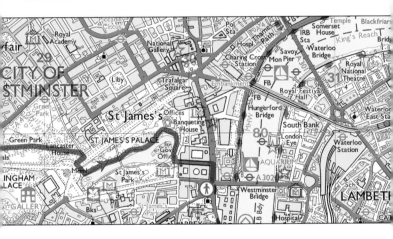

Over another pelican crossing, you enter **Green Park**. Take the path half-left, and then turn first right, coming to a path junction with a lamp-standard – from here, continue on the central of three paths leading forwards. When you reach the grand ceremonial avenue of The Mall, turn right, walking towards **Buckingham Palace**, home to the sovereign. In fact, this is the rear of the palace – its front overlooks a secluded garden with lake, where Royal garden parties are held. Cross The Mall at the pelican crossing and enter **St James's Park**.

Walk down to the lake and turn left, keeping the lake on your right, passing the Inn on the Park and circling round the head of the lake to the little cottage on Duck Island. Leave the park near here, cross the road, and go up the steps by the Clive memorial into King Charles Street, empty of traffic save for the occasional official car to the Foreign and Commonwealth Office or the Treasury, the two government departments which flank it. At the end is busy Whitehall; an entrance to **Westminster tube** is to your right, with the Houses of Parliament a little further on.

LONDON PLANE, *PLATANUS × HISPANICA*

London plane avenue, Kensington Gardens

With its ability to tolerate city air pollution and compacted earths, the London plane can reach a great height – 30m is common, equivalent to a 10-storey building. Its maple-like lush-green leaves, possessing what one London writer called 'otter-like sleekness', shrug off with ease all our climate can throw at it. If any tree could be designed for one city, the London plane could have been designed for London, and there's barely a part of the capital that is far from its benevolent shade.

And yet, is it a London tree at all? Somehow, the oriental plane of the Balkans was brought together with the American sycamore, perhaps in Spain, perhaps in the pleasure-grounds of Vauxhall Gardens in 17th-century London. Whichever it was, a hybrid resulted, although it harbours relatively little wildlife, so it is not perfection.

No London plane has yet been known to die of old age, but it faces grave threats. Massaria disease can lead to the shedding of larger branches. More serious still is the deadly, and apparently intractable, fungus *Ceratocystis platani*. It was introduced from America to 1940s Italy, and has spread slowly but unceasingly northwards since. Recently, it has caused thousands of trees to be felled from the banks of the Canal du Midi in southern France.

Walk 11
Hampstead Heath

In the 40 years leading to 1869, local landowner Sir Thomas Wilson put bill after bill before parliament to build over the core of Hampstead Heath. Thankfully all failed, and London has one of its great open spaces, a place celebrated in the verse of Keats and Coleridge and the art of Constable. The Heath is a magnificent refuge for wildlife, with grassland, bog, wood and hedgerow featuring as well as heath. A quarter of Britain's spider species can be found here.

Parliament Hill

Start/finish	Gospel Oak station (TQ 282 856)
Alternative start/finish	Hampstead tube (TQ 263 857)
Distance	6½ miles (11km); short cut 4½ miles (7km)
Time	3½hrs; short cut 2½hrs
Maps	OS Explorer 184, Landranger 168
Refreshments	Old Oak pub at the start; cafés near the start, Kenwood House, and Golders Hill Park; Jack Straw's Castle pub
Parking	Parliament Hill Lido, NW5 1LT
Local group	The Heath & Hampstead Society www.heathandhampstead.org.uk

The lime tree avenue near the Vale of Health

Humans may feel less welcoming when the night-time territorial screams disturb sleep. Some writers go further: 'Kill the revolting creatures', said commentator and west London resident Toby Young in *The Spectator*. In truth, road accidents and disease such as mange are as effective as the gun could ever be, for a city fox will be lucky to see its second birthday, whereas a rural fox might well live to be five or six, if not more.

The open spaces of Hampstead Heath, country within the city, with no doubt some very choice cast-off food in the affluent settlements around it, are prime ground for some of London's 10,000 foxes. However, the fox sunning itself in the photograph happens to be enjoying the author's garden in east London, a few steps from Walk 4.

The view from Parliament Hill

Walk 12

Dollis Valley Greenwalk

Way back in 1937, the Mayor of Finchley Alfred Pike had the enlightened idea of marking his borough's southern and western borders – the Mutton and Dollis brooks – with a path. Land was bought to safeguard the route, and today it has grown to become the Dollis Valley Greenwalk, a streamside stroll that takes you all the way from Hampstead to the open country near the Hertfordshire border. This walk could link with Walk 11, and it could also be split into two, with Totteridge and Whetstone tube serving as a breaking point.

Looking towards Gravel Pit wood, above Mount Moat open space

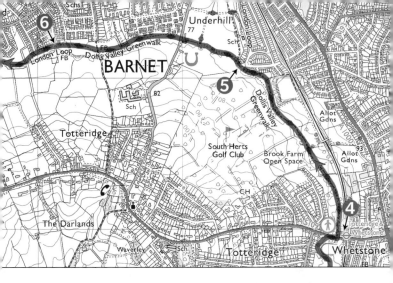

WILD GARLIC, *ALLIUM URSINUM*

In April and May, a double transformation comes on the woods and shaded streams of Britain, a transformation of both sight and scent. Turn a corner, and you might catch first a pungent whiff of garlic, and a moment later a wash of white, star-like flowers. You have come on a carpet of wild garlic, or to use one of its many folk-names ramsons. The Dollis Brook around the Windsor open space is just one place in London where you might find a stretch.

The leaves of wild garlic, which can be 25cm long, are grey-green, oval and narrow, and grow around the base of the stem. The white flowers form in star-like clusters at the head of the straight stems.

Flowers, leaves and bulbs are all edible, but foraging is not recommended at marginal sites such as Dollis Brook. The tiny bulbs are nothing like the size of those of culinary garlic, *Allium sativum*. The leaves, on the other hand, are endlessly versatile, for anything from a spinach or basil substitute to salad ingredient; the flowers, best picked young, have the added benefit of a cool beauty.

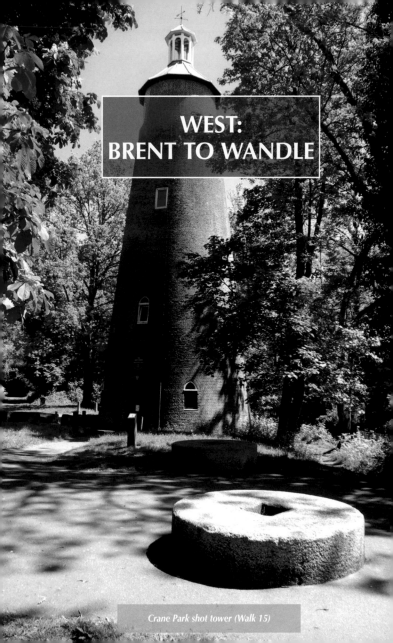

WEST:
BRENT TO WANDLE

Crane Park shot tower (Walk 15)

INTRODUCTION

Approaching Spanker's Hill (Walk 17)

There has long been an assumption that London's favoured west is the antithesis to its gritty east. The royal lands of Richmond, Home and Bushy parks form a great wedge across the Thames either side of Kingston. Richmond Park, and Ruislip Woods further north, form London's two national nature reserves; and the gardens at Kew are rightly a World Heritage Site of international botanic importance.

This may all be true, but denies the capacity of London, any part of London, to have inner complexities that challenge received opinion. Yes, the river is less industrial, but opposite Kew the Grand Union Canal joins it at the working town of Brentford. The boundary river of the Wandle was once one of the most heavily industrialised in Europe, but now something of a showpiece for restoration – although its tough aura is never far beneath the surface. On the other bank the Crane shows something similar. And what might London have been like if the doughty locals of Wimbledon had not battled to save their Common?

Walk 13

Ruislip Woods

These woods, the largest ancient semi-natural woodland in London, give a glimpse of how the ancient county of Middlesex used to be before the hand of man took effect. Enjoy the forest rides that penetrate the forest and the magnificent oak standards that tower high overhead. Between the two stretches of woodland, the area around the reservoir on the River Pinn, which is known as Ruislip Lido, has plenty of attractions – there's even a beach if you want to top up your tan!

In Mad Bess Wood

PENDUNCULATE OAK, *QUERCUS ROBUR*

This oak has played a major part in the English historical narrative, from the Royal Oak in which Charles II hid to the 'walls of oak' of the Royal Navy at the height of its power. But its role in the English landscape is even more dominant.

An ecosystem all by itself, the oak can support 400 insect species in its branches and, at its base, all manner of autumn fungi in the rich mulch produced by the fall of its half-million leaves. And yet that canopy is open enough for springtime light to create a carpet of bluebell and primrose below. Bats and birds nest in trunk holes.

The oak's timescale is beyond the understanding of our species: a half-century passes before the first acorns fall, growth slows only after 120 years, and 500 years elapse before the tree reaches old age – although coppicing or pollarding might double that.

The oak's wide tolerance of temperatures means that climate change is not a direct threat to its British range, unless summer droughts proliferate. There are threats, though, including the unpleasant oak processionary moth (you will see signs warning against it in the Richmond area) and a condition known as 'acute oak decline'. And 'pendunculate'? This denotes the acorn-stalk (peduncle), which the sessile oak does not have.

Walk 14

Yeading Brook

The upper reaches of the River Crane are known as the Yeading Brook; indeed, at 16 miles the brook is nearly twice the length of the river itself. Although long stretches near the source in Harrow are close to housing, the section covered in this walk goes through four nature reserves and a park, following (apart from one diversion) a quarter of west London's Hillingdon Trail. For a longer option, after completing this walk you could continue on to Walk 13, a route totalling 11 miles.

Ickenham Marsh

Start	Yeading Lane (TQ 111 821)
Finish	West Ruislip station (TQ 083 868)
Alternative finish	Ickenham tube (TQ 080 859)
Distance	5 miles (8km)
Time	2½hrs
Maps	OS Explorer 172 and 173, Landranger 176
Refreshments	Home Bar and Soldier's Return pubs in West Ruislip
Public transport	Bus E6 or 140 to Yeading from Hayes station or 140 from Northolt tube
Parking	West Ruislip station car park, HA4 7DW

From the Willow Tree Lane bus stop in Yeading walk to the end of Shakespeare Avenue. Ignore the footbridge but go through a gate and come out into **Yeading Brook Meadows**, part of which is still cut for hay each summer. Keep close to, but not beside, the brook – although there are one or two spots where you can pop over into the moist hollows surrounding it. At the next road, cross the brook, taking a bridleway past AFC Hayes football ground and then turning right ❶ at a waymark into Michael Frost Park. Just past a pond, take the path shown by the wooden 'HT' **Hillingdon Trail** waymarker. Turn right on a minor road (Charville Lane) and soon left to enter the nature reserve of **Ten Acre Wood** – although at 11ha, the wood is nearer 27 acres than 10.

Beyond Ten Acre Wood

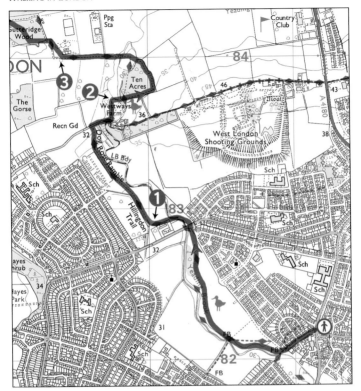

Known as **Golden Bridge**, the arc-shaped bridge opposite the entry to Ten Acre Wood is the latest in a series of bridges going back to at least 1754. Here in 1929, one of the last mass protests in London against the closure of rights of way took place. Among them was a young Bernard Miles, later leading British actor and peer. He returned in 1986 to open the present bridge.

Turn right on the flood relief bank ❷ for a few metres, then go down steps on the left to follow a path that goes round the right-hand edge of the wood. Don't worry if you hear gunfire – it comes from the very legal West London Shooting Grounds, safely behind the grassy banks to your right! Cross a footbridge, continue ahead over a pair of footbridges, then go left on a fenced path. Cross another pair of footbridges, and at the next stile, continue less claustrophobically on the right edge of the field until you can go through a gate ❸ on the right.

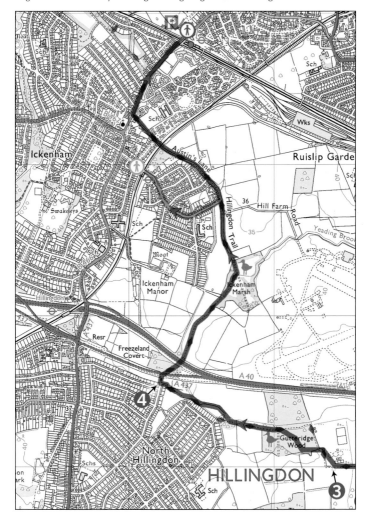

From here go half-left and enter **Gutteridge Wood**, following the Hillingdon Trail waymarkers as the path twists and turns until you are beside Yeading Brook again. Where the wood ends, keep houses and later a playground on your left, then follow the waymarkers by an allotment ❹ and under two roads. After the second, the busy **A40**, go ahead into a meadow, as rural an aspect as any on the whole walk. Veer right as it ends, into **Ickenham Marsh**. Don't cross the footbridge over the brook; our journey with it comes to an end but its course can be walked much of the way to its Harrow source.

The path becomes a rough track, **Austin's Lane**. Continue along it to the main road (Ickenham High Road) and turn right to reach **West Ruislip station**. You can join Walk 13 by crossing Ickenham High Road at the Soldier's Return pub. For Ickenham tube, turn left on to Glebe Avenue when you reach housing.

BANK VOLE, *MYODES GLAREOLUS*

Photo: Mammal Society

Crossing woodland, you might just catch sight of a blur of red and brown on the path beyond you. It could well be a bank vole, one of the most common mammals in Britain (population estimates in the tens of millions), although by no means one of the most sighted. Although it is not particularly secretive, the bank vole is more likely to be active after dusk and before dawn.

Areas like Ten Acre Wood and Gutteridge Wood are prime territory, for their mix of woodland and dense bramble gives cover from predators such as the fox, owl and kestrel. The bank vole lives underground (although it is also a prodigious climber and a good swimmer) in burrows made comfortable by moss and feathers and with separate larders for food, such as grasses, bark, fruits, nuts and seeds. It may also eat worms, spiders and even eggs.

Males and females keep distinct territories, and the territory of a male will encompass those of several females. Population numbers build up significantly over the summer breeding season, perhaps tripling. The female becomes sexually mature after six weeks, the male after eight, so with four to six litters possible a season, youngsters of the first litter can reproduce while later batches are still young.

Walk 15

Crane Park

This short Thames tributary follows a chequered course that includes a close encounter with Heathrow Airport and abandoned railway marshalling yards. However, some beautiful stretches remain, the part through Crane Park perhaps the finest. Once a frequent scene of explosive devastation, it now includes a splendid nature reserve.

River Crane

Start/finish	Whitton station (TQ 142 735)
Distance	4 miles (6km)
Time	2hrs
Maps	OS Explorer 161, Landranger 176
Refreshments	Cafés at Whitton and in Kneller Park, near the finish
Parking	Jubilee Avenue, TW2 6JA
Local group	Friends of the River Crane Environment www.force.org.uk

Turn left out of the station and walk down Percy Road, then left on to Hospital Bridge Road. Cross at the pelican crossing just after the **church** and bear right by the main road, ignoring the first entry on the right into Crane Park, crossing the river, and taking the second entry ❶. In a few metres turn right on a grass path. Continue ahead, ignoring forks, and go down steps soon leading to the riverbank.

At a road, turn right over the river and go immediately right on a path (before the second bridge). Continue, with the river never far away to your right, to a footbridge and then go immediately right. This leads to a more open area with the Shot Tower ❷ and a footbridge on to Crane Island.

The shot tower, which is open to the public on Sunday afternoons, is a remnant of **Hounslow Gunpowder Mills**. The mills were built in 1766 and were once among the largest gunpowder mills of Europe, with around 100 different buildings. The island is a creation of the mills, so that water power from the mill race could drive the machinery. Crack willow trees in the area were useful in producing charcoal; the largest in the country is said to grow here. Fatal explosions at the mills were frequent. Dickens' associate Richard H Horne described the aftermath of one such explosion in 1852: 'immense gaps in the fir groves, trees are reduced to half their height, some have been flayed of their bark all down one side'. The mills closed in 1926, and parts were sold off for the park that remains today.

Turn right over the two footbridges on to the island. At barely 2ha, it's simple to choose whichever informal paths you wish to explore the many habitats, from reedbed to meadow, millrace to woodland, but a simple circumnavigation will show them all. To do this turn right after the second footbridge to the concreted area at the western tip, and then continue along the southern bank (opposite the

FALLOW DEER, *DAMA DAMA*

The deer family are the largest British mammals, but only roe deer and red deer are natives; fallow deer were brought over to England by the Normans, for their meat and for sport, although they were also known to have been present in Roman times.

Many fallow deer have a tan-coloured coat with white spots, with a paler variety known as menil (also spotted), and another that is almost white. A black variety is the predominant variation in Epping Forest.

In the autumn rut, the bucks fight at dawn for dominance using their antlers, which are flattened ('palmate'), unlike the 16-pointed display of red deer or the barely foot-long antlers of the roe. Sometimes, one buck may take a harem of does; other times, a 'lek' of several bucks and a few does might form; and isolated bucks might wait for a doe, or pursue one.

Fallow deer are herbivorous, and left uncontrolled can strip large areas of vegetation. With no natural predators, numbers could soon denude Bushy and Richmond parks, and as a result there is night-time culling – males are culled just before the rut and females just after. The parks are closed while this takes place.

Continue through a paddock to another gate with the same name. To your right are the railings surrounding the formal gardens of Hampton Court Palace. Follow the railings to **The Long Water**, and turn left beside it. At the fountains at the head of the water, turn left inside the lime tree avenue, continue ahead when you cross a park road, and then fork half-right on a track, towards a church tower. Rejoin the road and leave the park at Kingston Gate ❺. Car drivers cross at the pelican crossing and go along Church Grove, entering Bushy Park at Hampton Wick Gate. Cross the main road at the zebra crossing and at the Swan pub veer left on to High Street before returning to **Hampton Wick station**.

Walk 17

Wimbledon Common and Richmond Park

Two of south-west London's great open spaces are covered in this walk. Richmond Park is immense by city standards, three times larger than New York's Central Park, and both a National Nature Reserve and European Special Area of Conservation, principally for its insect life. Yet Wimbledon Common is by no means outclassed by its neighbour – habitats include rare London bogland, and its preservation down the generations is an inspiring story on its own. This walk can be split into two shorter walks, breaking the route at Robin Hood Gate, which is a little under half way through.

Exercise ring, Wimbledon Common

planted in 1819. You soon pick up a grass path running half-right, which rises up the hill's low ridge. Just before the top, turn left on a thin path, which later contours just below the highest part of the hill (a little plateau guarded by sycamores and rhododendrons, if you wish to make your own way to the summit). The path takes you to a car park and the Pen Ponds café.

From the café, take the gravel path, and turn right on to a metalled lane. Just past a layby, turn half-left on a grass path. After crossing a horse-ride **4**, the path leads to a gate in the deer fence surrounding the **Isabella Plantation**. Enter the plantation here, stay near its right edge to Peg's Pond, and then turn left past a bench dedicated to Lady Rix. Lady Rix was a mental health campaigner and, as Elspet Gray, a successful post-war light comedy actor. Continue through the Heather Garden, a little stream soon on your right, and at a T-junction of gravelled paths turn right. Turn left past (seasonal) toilets and leave the plantation by a gate.

The area covered by the **Isabella Plantation** was first enclosed in 1831, to retain tree cover that would otherwise be lost to deer-nibbling. The present plantation dates only from 1950, with planting first by JM Fisher, the architect of Waterhouse Plantation in Bushy Park (Walk 16). Compared to the often empty spaces of the rest of the park, the plantation is something of a honeypot for those who love its displays of bluebells, camellias and rhododendrons.

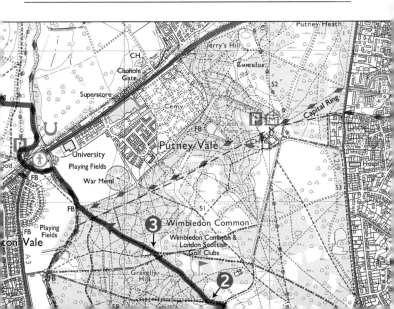

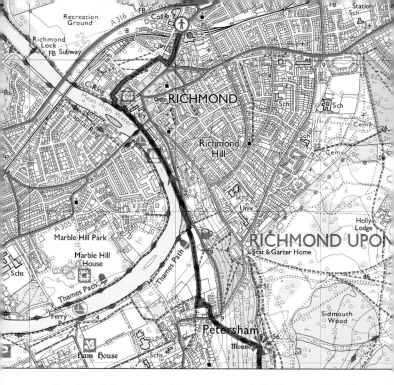

Turn right, fork next left, and in 100 metres go half-right on a path made narrow in summer by bracken. Ignore a crossing path and join a broad horse-ride. Cross the Park's perimeter road **⑤** and take the path which contours a little to the right above the valley dropping away below you. Go right at a tree stump that is about 2m high, still contouring – resist the temptation to drop down the scarp slope, or go up to join the road. At a signpost turn left on the Capital Ring, then veering right to go below **Pembroke Lodge** (its café can be accessed by a gate on the right) and soon a thatched cottage. Below this you can at last drop diagonally down the scarp, heading for the buildings of **Petersham.** Twickenham Stadium, home of English rugby union, is clearly seen in the middle distance.

Cross the road and follow the Capital Ring past a church and across Petersham Meadows to join the **River Thames**, and hence the Thames Path. Continue under Richmond Bridge and past the White Cross pub turn right on Friars Lane, then cross the right-hand edge of **Richmond Green**. Turn right into Duke Street and then take the second left to **Richmond station**.

The Thames Path keeps close to the park's boundary wall, past **Syon House** and a garden centre with café, before entering a wide alley which takes you to a main road at **Brentford**. Turn right, soon crossing the Grand Union Canal, which here is a navigation of the River Brent, and turn right on to The Ham at the Six Bells pub. This takes you through an industrial area – so different to the tree-lined rural walk on the other bank.

Thames Path signs lead you through its intricacies, first up steps immediately after an old railway bridge ❷, then two crossings of the canal (at Thames Lock, use the road and not the footbridge), back to Brentford High Street for a few metres, soon turning right again. This path too comes back to the High Street. Continue to the **Waterman Arts Centre** (ignore the 'Waterman's Park' alternative on your right), where you can rejoin the Thames proper for the first sustained stretch since Isleworth.

The path comes back to the road just once more, at the **Musical Museum**, before taking a right down steps signposted 'The Hollows', finally keeping between the river and new housing all the way back to Kew Bridge. The water tower on your left was built in the 1830s and now houses the London Museum of Water and Steam, with its collection of magnificent steam pumping engines (**www. waterandsteam.org.uk/**).

Go up the ramp on the left and look past the Express Tavern for Kew Bridge station. For Kew Gardens station, cross the bridge, continue on Kew Road and retrace your steps from the church.

BUFF-TAILED BUMBLEBEE, *BOMBUS TERRESTRIS*

The bumblebee's lazy swing from flower to flower, moving pollen from plant to plant and gathering nectar for the health of its hive, gives nature watchers one of their most hypnotic summer-time pleasures. Except that perhaps it is not summer, but November or even February. What is that bee doing there?

In London at any rate, you are seeing the buff-tailed bumblebee at work. Its winter foraging has been routinely observed in the capital since the start of the millennium, and two factors are at play: a bit more winter warmth, and suitable winter-flowering plants. Research by Kew showed that arbutus and mahonia shrubs, and the musk-willow, were among the principal plants visited by the bee in winter; they are frequently found in London's parks and gardens, precisely because they flourish in the late autumn and winter. It is relatively straightforward to identify this particular bee, the clue being in the name, although the queens' tails are sometimes nearly orange, and workers' are white with a buff line. They can sometimes be confused with the white-tailed bumblebee, *B. lucorum*, of similar size, but its queens have lemon-yellow bands on the abdomen, in contrast to the golden yellow of the buff-tailed variety. And you won't see the white-tailed in a London winter.

footpath 55 and keeping ahead over a minor road. Change banks at Hackbridge Road, taking footpath 61 then almost immediately footpath 62 by the river until you join a quiet road which in 200 metres passes the entrance **❻** to the nature reserve of Wilderness Island Nature Reserve – well worth a detour.

Wilderness Island, situated between the two arms of the Wandle, boasts ponds and wetlands, woods and wildflower meadows. It's one of the places you might spot a kingfisher – others include the wetlands of Morden Hall Park and the river south of Watermeads Nature Reserve – and there are three species of woodpecker here too. On the meadow look for the summertime lilac flowers of vervain and the small copper butterfly, or listen out for the crackle of Roesel's bush cricket.

Go under the railway and stay on Mill Lane to a path by the river. Take the second footbridge to enter The Grove with the river on your right, artificial rapids lending even more drama to the river. Take the waymarks first to Carshalton Ponds and then those towards Beddington Park, turning right at **Westcroft Leisure Centre** and then left on a road. From Elms Pond (fountain) cross the road to go along Lakeside, and keep ahead on a path.

Enter **Beddington Park** through a car park, looking for a footbridge over the Wandle, which you cross, turning right to keep beside the large pond which is here the river. It's soon a stream. Ignore a flint bridge **❼** to keep ahead on an

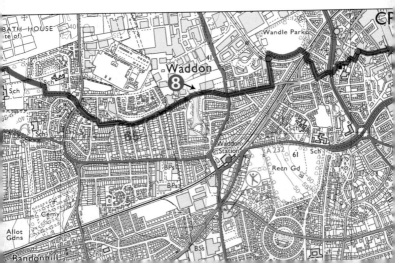

Terracotta bridge, Beddington Park

informal path through trees by the river. Change banks at the bridge after the distinctive terracotta bridge, and exit the park by a path running half-right across a field.

Over to your right, next to the church, is the Tudor house of **Carew Manor**, now a special school. The Grade I-listed hall retains its arch-braced hammer-beam roof, as also seen at Hampton Court, and one of the last in the country.

Turn left over the footbridge, then go half-right across a field, the path becoming metalled. Cross a pair of footbridges, turn left, cross the road at a pelican

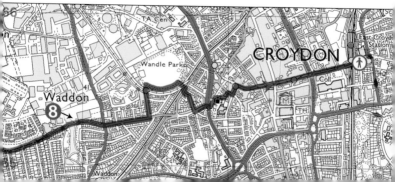

crossing and continue on footpath 99. Turn right on Bridle Path and continue on bridleway 100. You pass Waddon Ponds **8** on your right and continue along Mill Lane.

The trail once ended at Waddon Ponds but an extension into Croydon gives a last chance to see the river, albeit at the expense of some very urban walking. If you wanted, you could walk through the park here, and then Waddon station isn't far away. At the end of Mill Lane cross the main road, go along Waddon Road, and turn left into Vicarage Road, to enter **Wandle Park** past its tram stop. Here, in a grassy depression, is the last sight of the Wandle.

Leave the park just after the bandstand, go over a railway and take the little street by house 105; then turn left on footpath 617, right (Sylverdale Road), and left on St John's Road. Go through the subway, up the slope, and keep the **church** on your right, into an alley on your left just beyond. Go down Old Palace Road, then turn right to follow the tramway through Croydon's busy shopping area, noting the 16th-century Whitgift almshouses as you do, all the way to **East Croydon station**.

KINGFISHER, *ALCEDO ATTHIS*

Once you have seen a kingfisher, you know it could be nothing else. Its back bright-blue, its breast orange, sweeping fast above the water, it is utterly distinctive and something of an emblem in a city where colour is sometimes in short supply. That a good number of the 4000 or so pairs breeding in Britain do so in cities in general, and London in particular, is a testament to the work done in cleaning up urban lands.

Photo: Peter Rowe

Find a kingfisher and you have found fresh water. That you can do so by the Wandle, which in living memory was essentially a sewer, is nothing short of remarkable. Because the kingfisher is a diving bird, it needs to enter water that is clean, not murky, first so it can see its prey when flying at speed and then to home in on it when it is beneath the surface, eyes protected by a transparent third eyelid. It can swallow a 10-cm fish whole, no mean feat when its own body length is only around 15cm, but will take insects too.

The kingfisher is highly territorial, controlling half a mile or so of river. Nests are generally made in the riverbank, although on the Wandle, concrete pipes have been pressed into use.

SOUTH:
EAST OF THE WANDLE

The view from Addington Hill (Walk 21)

INTRODUCTION

Downland hanger, east of Downe (Walk 25)

South of the River Thames lies London's undiscovered country, at least if you talk to anyone who lives north of the river. But if south is different from north, then there is a good reason for it, in terms of human geography. Because the tube system pokes only one long finger into south London, it's largely absent from the tube map, and so it's out of mind to those who navigate by that Harry Beck masterpiece.

The tube ventures so rarely south because its preferred tunnelling medium, London clay, is less prevalent here. Instead there are sands, gravels and, above all – the further south you go – chalk. These bring with them a range of low hills, some essentially just isolated outcrops, others linked to one of the great chalk ranges of southern England, the North Downs. In the inner city, a chain of woodlands occupies some of those outcrops; beyond, the city merges seamlessly into the farmlands of west Kent and north Surrey. And as we shall see in the final walk of this collection, this countryside was to be the setting for one of the great advances in human thought, intimately linked to the detailed study of its plant and animal life.

Walk 20
Happy Valley

There's a little patch of downland, an extension of the North Downs, that creeps into south London, and here is a walk that shows it off well, with steep scarp slopes and a typical dry 'hanger' valley. In spring there are beautiful wildflower meadows, and although you can choose to shorten the walk, this option misses the remarkable church at Chaldon.

Above Happy Valley

Walk 21
Hills and woods of Croydon

Croydon town centre is noted for brutalist, road-orientated town planning, but head to the outer parts of the borough and it has some very fine countryside, peppered with nature reserves. Enjoy one of the great London views from Addington Hill, some of the best London woods at Selsdon, and finally the closest chalk downland to the centre of the city, with the orchid-friendly site of Hutchinson's Bank at the finish.

Hutchinson's Bank

Start	East Croydon station (TQ 328 657)
Finish	New Addington tram stop (TQ 381 622)
Distance	7 miles (11km)
Time	3½hrs
Maps	OS Explorer 161, Landranger 177
Refreshments	At East Croydon; café at Coombe Wood
Parking	North Downs Road, New Addington, CR0 0LF
Local group	Friends of Selsdon Wood www.friendsofselsdonwood.co.uk

Cross the tram tracks and go down Altyre Road, signposted for the courts. At the end, cross the main road by the pelican crossing and turn half-left on Fairfield

Path. Turn right leaving Cotelands ❶, then left on to St Bernards. Keep heading south-easterly on the path through a couple of estates, often waymarked for the Vanguard Way. Finally, you come out at **Lloyd Park**.

Here, look for a waymark post by railings just to your left, and walk ahead across the grass, heading past a play area before veering right to cross the tramway and turning left beside a road. Where the Vanguard Way turns right at Coombe Wood, instead go half-left on Oaks Road, and just before a thatched cottage go right on a path into woods. In 250 metres take a path left ❷, then at the fourth path junction in a further 300 metres turn right. After this, the next path left takes you up steps to **Addington Hill**.

ADDINGTON HILL

Addington Hill, or Hills? Even the Ordnance Survey can't make its mind up over singular or plural, depending on the scale. Essentially, the hills (collectively) form a gravel-based heathland plateau, in the centre of which two spurs run north to give what look like high points, although they aren't. This walk ascends the more easterly of these near-arêtes, and it's a wonderful viewpoint. Late summer is a good time to be here, to see the heather at its purple-blooming best.

Here, you join the London Loop by taking the wide path running south-east, following the Loop's waymarks – the first is just before a car park. Cross the tramway at the Coombe Lane stop and turn left on the path between tramway and road, soon crossing over into **Heathfield**. With trams running frequently from Coombe Lane to both start and finish of the walk, it's easy to break the walk here. The Loop leads you down and up steps through this ornamental garden and into **Bramley Bank Nature Reserve**. When you leave the reserve, go right, but don't join the cul-de-sac, instead going up into **Littleheath Woods**. In a meadow, veer left of a birch tree group ❸, and soon merge back onto the **Vanguard Way**, which here coincides with the Loop.

Veer right just before housing. Out of the woods, cross a road at a bus stop and walk down Ashen Vale, soon taking a path behind houses which leads you into **Selsdon Wood**, noticing the chalk beneath your feet. Continue on the Loop for 120 metres but at the first path crossroads leave it by turning right on to Broad Walk. When you come out to a meadow, cross it half-left and then veer left ❹, soon coming to another meadow. Cross this also, and take the path running half-left. Ignore three crossing paths, but turn right at the fourth.

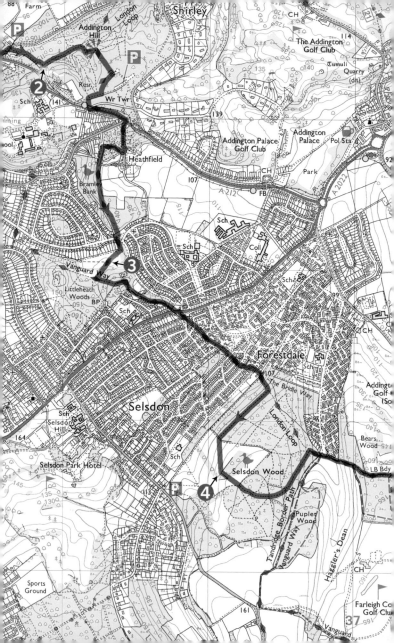

The way into Selsdon Wood

Like the woodlands near Chislehurst (Walk 24), **Selsdon Wood** was saved for posterity by a mix of wealthy benefactors and what we now call crowd-funding, with small donations from more than 10,000 individuals in the 1920s and 1930s. A nature reserve since 1936, the wood is now owned by the National Trust and includes spacious hay meadows as well as oak, beech and ash woodland, and hazel coppice.

At the edge of the woods, the London Loop and Vanguard Way (which you briefly rejoined) turn right, but the walk instead goes ahead on another bridleway. Climb up a downland scarp slope, but at the top take care not to contour right with the bridleway. Instead fork left on a thin path into **Frith Wood**, which brings you out to a fence on the left. There are occasional waymarks for the Tandridge Border Path – in fact, you are a few feet over the Surrey side of the London border. Go left at a path junction and you come to a road.

Cross it and enter Farleigh Dean Crescent, but only for a few metres until you take **Featherbed Lane** on the right. Soon go left through a gate into **Hutchinson's Bank**. On this downland slope can be found 100 species of moth, 28 of butterfly, and orchids and rare grasses too. Keep a fence surrounding new planting on your right and then turn left on the third path. Climb on this to the top of the bank, and then turn left on the crossing path just beyond double gates. Turn right when you come to a metalled path. At housing, go left on the road, and almost immediately right on a green space between houses. **New Addington tram stop** is just beyond the gorilla statue, and all trams from this stop go to East Croydon station.

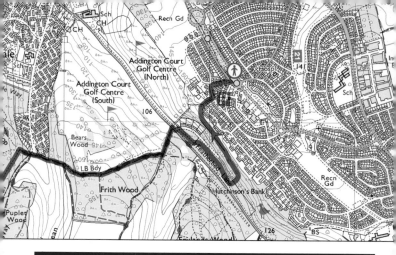

PYRAMIDAL ORCHID, *ANACAMPTIS PYRAMIDALIS*

How would Charles Darwin follow up his paradigm-shifting work *On the Origin of Species*? With *Fertilisation of Orchids* (1862), in which the pyramidal orchid was an exemplar species.

Sheltered by a petal, the stamen of a pyramidal orchid contains pollen masses joined to adhesive balls combined into a strap or saddle shape. When a moth or butterfly inserts its proboscis, pollen is deposited on it, which is transferred to the stigma of the next pyramidal orchid the insect visits, and pollination thus achieved. Darwin's studies showed how this microscopic action varies between orchids, and – crucially – requires orchids and their pollinators to co-evolve. One particular Madagascan orchid is now known as Darwin's orchid, as he predicted the nature of the pollinating moth many decades before it was known to science.

Like many orchids, the pyramidal orchid can be erratic from year to year, as the seeds need additional nourishment from specific soil fungi, which if not present will mean less flowering. Although the flowers of most pyramidal orchids are purple, some are white, and a few pink. The pyramidal orchid can certainly be seen on this walk, and several others too. Darwin's research was, in fact, carried out not far away, on the 'orchis bank' of Walk 25.

OXLEAS WOOD

Parts of this wood date back 8000 years, to the end of the last Ice Age. Oak, hornbeam and silver birch predominate, alongside some excellent examples of the wild service tree. Many trees are around 900 years old. London's rarest native amphibian, the palmate newt, survives here. Plants such as wood anemone, wood sorrel and bluebell are a good indication of the wood's antiquity, and rare rushes and fungi have a home here too. With Jack Wood and Shepherdleas Wood it constitutes the Oxleas Woodlands Site of Special Scientific Interest, and these plus Eltham Common make up a nature reserve.

You might think that such a large area of unspoilt woodland, one of the few to have survived in this or any other part of London, would be sacrosanct from destructive development. However, in 1979 Oxleas Wood lay in the path of a planned dual carriageway link road from a new Thames bridge to the A2. Two separate public enquiries recommended a tunnel: the Department of Transport ignored both. Years of protest, marked by schemes such as 'adopt-a-tree' and international postcard campaigns as well as weighty legal argument, followed until the plan was withdrawn in 1993.

Beyond the café, enter **Oxleas Wood**, dropping down to a shallow ditch with a prominent signpost and, almost all the time, parakeets screeching above you. There's a direct line to Falconwood station by turning right, but that exits this fine wood far too quickly. Instead turn left for 130 metres and then turn right at a litter bin. Turn right again in 200 metres and just over a ditch go half-right at the path junction. At the next junction keep ahead, on the thinner of two paths, until you reach another Green Chain/Capital Ring waymarker. Turn left here, and over Rochester Way enter Shepherdleas Wood. When the Green Chain splits once more, continue ahead, signed for **Falconwood station**, which is just over the main road you soon meet.

RING-NECKED PARAKEET, *PSITTACULA KRAMERI*

Photo: Tony Morrison

Jimi Hendrix in the 1960s? The filmset of *The African Queen* in the 1950s? Nazi bombing of London zoo in the 1940s? Or just a cage door inadvertently open, maybe back in the 1890s?

Almost the best thing about the ring-necked parakeet's hold on London skies is the myths about its original release. What is certain is that this invasive species has made itself very much at home in the capital, competing with native species for tree-hole nest sites. The parakeets are not yet so numerous that they can denude fields of crops, as in their native south Asia, but already they have official status as a pest.

Yet the parakeet has its defenders. Many enjoy, if not the squawking cry, the hint of the exotic that it brings from its red bill and bright green body, and perhaps the sheer otherness of its shape. They point to the uneasy extension of the debate to the establishment of new human communities in a city that has always been outward-facing to the world. But if the parakeet's creation myths are almost the best thing about it, from the point of view of the owl or peregrine, there is one thing better. Those raptors find that the parakeet makes an excellent meal.

APPENDIX B

Where to find out more

For tourist information in London, the official website is www.visitlondon.com. They have many tourist information centres across the capital. For more information about wildlife in London and its 40 plus nature reserves, go to the website of the London Wildlife Trust www.wildlondon.org.uk.

Responsibility for other reserves and open spaces is split between a wide range of bodies, including:

- all 32 London boroughs (the pan-London Greater London Authority has strategic powers)
- the City of London Corporation, which manages Epping Forest, Hampstead Heath, Farthing Downs and many other open spaces, www.cityoflondon.gov.uk
- the Royal Parks www.royalparks.org.uk
- the National Trust www.nationaltrust.org.uk

There is of course plenty of information on the web, just an internet search away, but don't forget traditional media. Most major and independent London bookshops have sections devoted to the capital, and will be a far more rewarding way of scoping the vast array of its literature than trying to branch out from 'Customers who bought this item…' on Amazon. Stanfords in Covent Garden specialises in books and maps for walkers.

Three works that have been invaluable in writing this guide are:

- Andrew Crowe, *The Parks and Woodlands of London* (Fourth Estate, 1987) – out of print, but might be found in second-hand shops
- Richard Jefferies, *Nature Near London* (1883) – available via www.general-books.net
- Marianne Taylor, *Watching Wildlife in London* (New Holland, 2010) – a valuable complement to this guide to find out some of the best sites for particular species

Authors such as Peter Ackroyd and Iain Sinclair write with great insight on the (psycho-)geography of London, while don't ignore Charles Dickens, for whom London was as much a character in his works as Oliver Twist or David Copperfield.

Three other Cicerone titles also include walks in London:

- Leigh Hatts, *The Lea Valley Walk* (2015)
- Leigh Hatts, *The Thames Path* (2016)
- Peter Aylmer, *Walking in Essex* (2013). Includes three walks in east London and a traverse of Epping Forest.

DOWNLOAD THE ROUTE
IN GPX FORMAT

All the routes in this guide are available for download from:

www.cicerone.co.uk/813/GPX

as GPX files. You should be able to load them into most formats of mobile device, whether GPS or smartphone.

When you go to this link, you will be asked for your email address and where you purchased the guide, and have the option to subscribe to the Cicerone e-newsletter.

www.cicerone.co.uk

LISTING OF CICERONE GUIDES

SCOTLAND

Backpacker's Britain:
   Northern Scotland
Ben Nevis and Glen Coe
Cycling in the Hebrides
Great Mountain Days in Scotland
Mountain Biking in Southern and
   Central Scotland
Mountain Biking in West and
   North West Scotland
Not the West Highland Way
   Scotland
Scotland's Best Small Mountains
Scotland's Mountain Ridges
Scrambles in Lochaber
The Ayrshire and Arran Coastal
   Paths
The Border Country
The Borders Abbeys Way
The Cape Wrath Trail
The Great Glen Way
The Great Glen Way Map Booklet
The Hebridean Way
The Hebrides
The Isle of Mull
The Isle of Skye
The Skye Trail
The Southern Upland Way
The Speyside Way
The Speyside Way Map Booklet
The West Highland Way
Walking Highland Perthshire
Walking in Scotland's Far North
Walking in the Angus Glens
Walking in the Cairngorms
Walking in the Ochils, Campsie
   Fells and Lomond Hills
Walking in the Pentland Hills
Walking in the Southern Uplands
Walking in Torridon
Walking Loch Lomond and the
   Trossachs
Walking on Arran
Walking on Harris and Lewis
Walking on Rum and the Small
   Isles
Walking on the Orkney and
   Shetland Isles
Walking on Uist and Barra
Walking the Corbetts Vol 1 South
   of the Great Glen
Walking the Corbetts Vol 2 North
   of the Great Glen
Walking the Munros
   Vol 1 – Southern, Central and
   Western Highlands
Walking the Munros
   Vol 2 – Northern Highlands
   and the Cairngorms

West Highland Way Map Booklet
Winter Climbs Ben Nevis and
   Glen Coe
Winter Climbs in the Cairngorms

NORTHERN ENGLAND TRAILS

Hadrian's Wall Path
Hadrian's Wall Path Map Booklet
Pennine Way Map Booklet
The Coast to Coast Map Booklet
The Coast to Coast Walk
The Dales Way
The Dales Way Map Booklet
The Pennine Way

LAKE DISTRICT

Cycling in the Lake District
Great Mountain Days in the Lake
   District
Lake District Winter Climbs
Lake District: High Level and
   Fell Walks
Lake District: Low Level and
   Lake Walks
Mountain Biking in the Lake
   District
Outdoor Adventures with
   Children – Lake District
Scrambles in the Lake District
   – North
Scrambles in the Lake District
   – South
Short Walks in Lakeland
   Book 1: South Lakeland
Short Walks in Lakeland
   Book 2: North Lakeland
Short Walks in Lakeland
   Book 3: West Lakeland
The Cumbria Way
Tour of the Lake District
Trail and Fell Running in the Lake
   District

NORTH WEST ENGLAND
AND THE ISLE OF MAN

Cycling the Pennine Bridleway
Cycling the Way of the Roses
Isle of Man Coastal Path
The Lancashire Cycleway
The Lune Valley and Howgills
The Ribble Way
Walking in Cumbria's Eden Valley
Walking in Lancashire
Walking in the Forest of Bowland
   and Pendle
Walking on the Isle of Man
Walking on the West Pennine
   Moors
Walks in Ribble Country
Walks in Silverdale and Arnside

NORTH EAST ENGLAND,
YORKSHIRE DALES
AND PENNINES

Great Mountain Days in the
   Pennines
Mountain Biking in the Yorkshire
   Dales
South Pennine Walks
St Oswald's Way and
   St Cuthbert's Way
The Cleveland Way and the
   Yorkshire Wolds Way
The Cleveland Way Map Booklet
The North York Moors
The Reivers Way
The Teesdale Way
Trail and Fell Running in the
   Yorkshire Dales
Walking in County Durham
Walking in Northumberland
Walking in the North Pennines
Walking in the Yorkshire Dales:
   North and East
Walking in the Yorkshire Dales:
   South and West
Walks in Dales Country
Walks in the Yorkshire Dales

WALES AND WELSH BORDERS

Glyndwr's Way
Great Mountain Days in
   Snowdonia
Hillwalking in Shropshire
Hillwalking in Wales – Vol 1
Hillwalking in Wales – Vol 2
Mountain Walking in Snowdonia
Offa's Dyke Map Booklet
Offa's Dyke Path
Ridges of Snowdonia
Scrambles in Snowdonia
The Ascent of Snowdon
The Ceredigion and Snowdonia
   Coast Paths
The Pembrokeshire Coast Path
Pembrokeshire Coast Path Map
   Booklet
The Severn Way
The Snowdonia Way
The Wales Coast Path
The Wye Valley Walk
Walking in Carmarthenshire
Walking in Pembrokeshire
Walking in the Forest of Dean
Walking in the South Wales
   Valleys
Walking in the Wye Valley
Walking on the Brecon Beacons
Walking on the Gower

For full information on all our
guides, books and eBooks,
visit our website:
www.cicerone.co.uk

Walking – Trekking – Mountaineering – Climbing – Cycling

Over 40 years, Cicerone have built up an outstanding collection of over 300 guides, inspiring all sorts of amazing adventures.

Every guide comes from extensive exploration and research by our expert authors, all with a passion for their subjects. They are frequently praised, endorsed and used by clubs, instructors and outdoor organisations.

All our titles can now be bought as **e-books**, **ePubs** and **Kindle** files and we also have an online magazine – **Cicerone Extra** – with features to help cyclists, climbers, walkers and trekkers choose their next adventure, at home or abroad.

Our website shows any **new information** we've had in since a book was published. Please do let us know if you find anything has changed, so that we can publish the latest details. On our **website** you'll also find great ideas and lots of detailed information about what's inside every guide and you can buy **individual routes** from many of them online.

It's easy to keep in touch with what's going on at Cicerone by getting our monthly **free e-newsletter**, which is full of offers, competitions, up-to-date information and topical articles. You can subscribe on our home page and also follow us on **Facebook** and **Twitter** or dip into our **blog**.

Cicerone – the very best guides for exploring the world.

CICERONE

Juniper House, Murley Moss, Oxenholme Road, Kendal, Cumbria LA9 7RL
Tel: 015395 62069 info@cicerone.co.uk
www.cicerone.co.uk and **www.cicerone-extra.com**